Novels for Students, Volume 41

Project Editor: Sara Constantakis **Rights Acquisition and Management**: Mary Snell, Robyn Young **Composition**: Evi Abou-El-Seoud **Manufacturing**: Rhonda Dover

Imaging: John Watkins

Product Design: Pamela A. E. Galbreath, Jennifer Wahi **Content Conversion**: Katrina Coach **Product Manager**: Meggin Condino © 2013 Gale, Cengage Learning

For product information and technology assistance, contact us at **Gale Customer Support, 1-800-877-4253.**

For permission to use material from this text or product, submit all requests online at **www.cengage.com/permissions**.

Further permissions questions can be emailed to **permissionrequest@cengage.com** While every effort has been made to ensure the reliability of the information presented in this publication, Gale, a part of Cengage Learning, does not guarantee the accuracy of the data contained herein. Gale accepts no payment for listing; and inclusion in the publication of any organization, agency, institution, publication, service, or individual does not imply endorsement of the editors or publisher. Errors brought to the attention of the publisher and verified to the satisfaction of the publisher will be corrected in future editions.

Gale
27500 Drake Rd.
Farmington Hills, MI, 48331-3535

ISBN-13: 978-1-4144-9484-5
ISBN-10: 1-4144-9484-X
ISSN 1094-3552

This title is also available as an e-book.

ISBN-13: 978-1-4144-9270-4
ISBN-10: 1-4144-9270-7
Contact your Gale, a part of Cengage Learning sales representative for ordering information.

Printed in Mexico
1 2 3 4 5 6 7 16 15 14 13 12

When the Emperor Was Divine

Julie Otsuka

2002

Introduction

When the Emperor Was Divine is a novel by American author Julie Otsuka that was published in 2002. Otsuka's first novel, it tells the story of the internment of Japanese Americans during World War II from 1942 to 1945. They were interned because the U.S. government thought they would be sympathetic to the Japanese cause and likely to participate in espionage or sabotage.

The story focuses on one family in particular, a mother and her two young children who are compelled to leave their home in California in the spring of 1942. They are sent to an internment camp in the remote desert at Topaz, in Utah. The father of the family was arrested in December 1941, immediately after the Japanese attack on Pearl Harbor, and his story forms part of the novel, too.

In a matter-of-fact, unemotional tone, Otsuka shows how Japanese Americans coped with the shock of being uprooted from their homes and forced to live in a makeshift camp with few amenities. The novel is valuable not only for the human story it tells but as a contribution to understanding an episode in U.S. history that is now universally regarded as a mistake and an injustice.

Author Biography

Otsuka was born on May 15, 1962, in Palo Alto, California, to Japanese American parents. Her father was an aerospace engineer and her mother a lab technician. The family moved to Palos Verdes, California, when Otsuka was nine. She excelled in high school and attended Yale University, graduating in 1984 with a BA in art. She was particularly interested in painting and sculpture, and for several years tried to make a living at it while also working as a waitress. She entered an MFA program at Indiana University in 1987 but left the program after only three months. She moved to New York but, within a couple of years, abandoned her goal of becoming a painter. Instead, she began reading American literature widely and writing some sketches of her own. As her interest in writing developed, she enrolled in an MFA program at Columbia University in 1994. She graduated in 1999, having completed much of the work that would within a few years become her first novel, *When the Emperor Was Divine*, which was published by Knopf in 2002. The subject matter, the internment of Japanese Americans during World War, was a historical event that had affected her own family: her grandparents, her mother—then eleven years old—and her uncle had been sent away from their homes to an internment camp in Topaz, Utah, during World War II. They spent three years at the camp.

When the Emperor Was Divine received many glowing reviews and was named a *New York Times* Notable Book, a *San Francisco Chronicle* Best Book of the Year, and a Barnes & Noble Discover Great New Writers finalist.

Otsuka's second novel, *The Buddha in the Attic*, was published in 2011. It is about the Japanese "picture brides" who came to the United States in the early 1900s in order to marry men whom they knew only through photographs.

As of 2012, Otsuka lives in New York City. She writes on her website that she spends the afternoons writing in her neighborhood café.

Evacuation Order No. 19

When the Emperor Was Divine begins in Berkeley, California, in the spring of 1942. The United States has entered World War II the previous December. A middle-aged Japanese American woman sees a notice in a post office window stating that all Japanese Americans must leave their homes by a certain date. She begins packing immediately, and nine days later, she is still packing. She goes to a hardware store to buy a few supplies and then tries to find a duffel bag for sale, but all the stores are sold out. She goes home and decides she must finish packing, and she takes some things from the rooms of her ten-year-old daughter and seven-year-old son, wraps them up and puts them in boxes. The family has to leave the next day and they do not know where they are going. The woman's husband was arrested the previous December following the Japanese attack on Pearl Harbor and is now imprisoned in Texas.

The woman gives their cat away, kills the chicken, and then kills and buries the pet dog. When the children come home, she tells them that tomorrow they will only be allowed to take with them what they can carry. After the children have gone to bed, the woman releases their bird, a macaw, from its cage. That night the woman lies awake worrying about the leaky roof of the house.

Train

It is September 1942; this chapter is told from the point of view of the woman's daughter. The family is on a train, moving through Nevada, with other Japanese Americans. For the last two and a half months the family had been staying at an assembly center at Tanforan, a racetrack near San Francisco. Now they are on their way to the Utah desert where they will be living in a camp. It is a Sunday and as they pass through a small town, the girl looks out the window until a soldier tells her to put the shades down, which they must do whenever they pass through a town. She talks briefly with another passenger, a man named Ted Ishimoto. She tells him that her father is in Lordsburg, New Mexico, and that he never writes to her, although the latter statement is not true; he sends her postcards every week and she saves them all. The girl then observes some other passengers, talks to her mother, and looks out the window again. Now that they are out of the town, the shades have been raised again. She tries to play cards with her brother, but he is not interested. Her mother gives her brother an orange to eat, while the girl slips all the cards, one by one, out the window. When her brother sleeps, she looks at the postcards her father has sent. Part of what he wrote has been blacked out by government censors.

She tries to sleep but is awakened in the

evening by the sound of breaking glass. Someone has thrown a brick through the window. She tells her mother she dreamt of her father.

They reach Utah at night. At a town called Delta, all the passengers get off the train and are put on buses that take them to the camp at Topaz, in the desert. The girl sees barbed-wire fences and soldiers.

When the Emperor Was Divine

It is late summer 1942 in the internment camp. It is hot and dry, and the wind blows up dust. The family adapts to the daily rhythms of their new home, in which the three of them live in one sparsely furnished room in a barrack. The boy misses his father. His mother tells him not to touch the barbed-wire fence or mention the Japanese emperor's name, but sometimes he whispers the name. The family passes the time as best they can, waiting for the mail and waiting for meals. They have no idea how long the war will last. The boy has nightmares and wonders whether he has done something bad that resulted in his being in the camp.

They receive censored letters from their father from Lordsburg. The boy sends replies and remembers his past interactions with his father. The boy hates the dust that is everywhere in the camp. Sometimes, in the evening, he and his sister go walking at the edge of the barracks to watch the sun set over the mountains.

In the fall, some of the people in the camp are recruited to work on farms in Idaho or Wyoming. When they return, they tell of the prejudice and abuse they encountered there. In the camp, the internees hear all kinds of wild rumors about what may happen to them, including being sterilized, shot, or deported to Japan.

A school opens in the camp in mid-October in an unheated barrack. The boy misses his father and remembers the night his father was taken away by the authorities. He remembers how, after that, curfews were imposed on Japanese American residents, as well as restrictions on how far they could travel.

There are dust storms in the fall, and snow falls as winter approaches. There is not much to do. There are rumors of spies in the camp, people who are thought to be government informers. In late November, some willow saplings are planted in the camp, and the boy takes a green leaf from one of them and sends it to his father.

The weather gets extremely cold. A man disappears and is found three days later frozen to death. At Christmas, turkey is served, as well as gifts for the children from the Quakers and the American Friends Service Committee. It is a long cold winter, and there is not enough bedding provided to stay warm at night. Illness is common. The boy's mother gets depressed and loses her appetite.

In February, army recruiters arrive looking for

volunteers who will be willing to take a test of loyalty to the United States. In spring, the boy starts to take long walks on his own. In April, a man is shot dead near the border fence. The guard says the man was trying to escape, but many do not believe this. His funeral is attended by nearly 2,000 people.

The long hot summer arrives. The boy thinks of the day when his father will return.

In a Stranger's Backyard

In fall 1945, after the war has ended, the family returns to their home in Berkeley. The house has been neglected. The paint is peeling and most of their furniture is gone. They do not know who lived in the house while they were away. Outside, the town seems much the same but when they meet people they know in the street, those people turn away and pretend not to have seen them. Someone throws a whiskey bottle through a window of their home.

Gradually, the men from the neighborhood who fought in the war come home. Some of them who were prisoners of war in Japan have harsh things to say about the Japanese. The children's old friends from school no longer invite them home for supper. The boy and the girl respond to hostility or indifference at school by just keeping to themselves, careful not to cause any trouble. All this is quite different from the friendly reception they thought they would receive.

By November, the family is poor and the

mother is turned down for almost every job she applies for. She ends up cleaning houses for a living and taking in people's washing and ironing to make extra money.

Their father finally returns in December. He looks much older, and the children can hardly believe he really is their father. He never says a word about what happened to him during his imprisonment. He is suspicious of people, and when he is outside, he does not speak unless spoken to. Small things make him lose his temper, but he is always pleased to see his children. When spring comes, he spends more and more time alone in his room. The children's lives gradually return to normal, and they face less hostility at school.

Confession

This short chapter is narrated in the first person by the father, who gives an account of what happened to him after he was taken away at night. In detention, he was told he had to talk to his interrogators. He gives a mock account of what happened, saying he admitted to being an enemy saboteur. He creates an absurd scenario in which he says he is guilty of everything from poisoning food to blowing up railroads, spying on airfields and neighbors, and many other things that are even more fantastic. He says he is like all the other Japanese in California who his interrogators know, and against whom they are prejudiced, thus implying that all the Japanese are guilty, a claim that he knows is absurd and will sound absurd. His bitterness is plain from his tone. Finally, having admitted to everything, he asks if he can go home.

Daughter

The daughter is ten years old in 1942 when the family is first sent to the internment camp. Unlike her parents, she was born in America and has always lived in California. She has straight black hair and is as American as any other girl her age. She likes "Boys and black licorice and Dorothy Lamour" (Lamour was a movie star at the time) as well as her pet macaw. She pays attention at school, studies for tests, and also takes piano lessons. She is good at drawing and has won a school prize for her work. Her world changes completely when the she and her mother and brother are sent away. Like her brother, she misses her father, and once confesses to her brother that what worries her most is that sometimes she cannot remember his face. She matures physically during the three years she spends at the camp, and when she undresses at night, she asks her brother to look the other way. She also gets to hear about some of the less savory things that go on at the camp during the nighttime hours. Sometimes she gets up in the middle of the night and jumps rope. She goes dancing in the evenings and wins second prize in a jitter-bug contest in the mess hall, where she also takes part in games of bingo.

When she, her mother, and her brother return

to their home in California after the war, they find they are shunned. At school, the other students will not sit with the girl or boy at lunchtime, and their old friends longer invite them to their homes for supper. The girl and her brother try to keep quiet and not bring attention to themselves. She goes out of her way to make sure she does not offend anyone.

Father

Before he is arrested by the authorities shortly after the Japanese attack on Pearl Harbor, the father, who like the other main characters is never identified by name, worked for a company. What he did for that company is never stated, but it obviously provided sufficient financial reward for him to establish a middle-class lifestyle for his wife and two children. The father was born in Japan, it would appear, and immigrated to the United States, where he must have lived for over twenty years. He is described as a "small handsome man with delicate hands and a raised white scar on his index finger." He dressed well, was always polite and punctual, and loved to play with the children. He also loved his adopted country; he once told his son that what he "loved most about America … was the glazed jelly donut."

The charges made against the father are never revealed. He is detained in a prison at Lordsburg for four years, during which time he writes affectionate letters to his children. He is finally released and returns home in December 1945, but he is far from the handsome, strong man his children knew. He has aged considerably in the four years he has been away. He is thin and bald, and he has lost all his teeth.

He is completely shattered by his experience of being imprisoned. He refuses to talk about it and never mentions politics. His personality has also deteriorated, and he has become suspicious and uncommunicative. Sometimes he will fly into a rage at the slightest provocation. His affection for his children remains, but he is a broken figure, retreating often to his room just to be alone. Sometimes he goes to bed as early as seven o'clock, immediately after supper.

Ted Ishimoto

Ted Ishimoto is a Japanese American man who is on the same train as the family as they travel to the internment camp. He has a friendly chat with the daughter.

Mrs. Kato

Mrs. Kato is an old Japanese American woman who lives in the internment camp. She lives with her son and his wife in the room next to the family. She talks to herself all the time and is confused about the situation she is in.

Mother

The mother of the two children was born in Japan into a large family. She had six older sisters and a younger brother. She has lived in the United States for nearly nineteen years in 1942. In the spring of 1942 she is forty-one years old, eleven years younger than her husband. By the standards of the day she had married late and had her children late, when she was in her thirties.

She is a practical woman who absorbs the shock of having her husband taken from her by the FBI and takes the necessary steps to ensure the family's smooth departure after she sees the relocation notice. She gives the cat away, kills and buries the family dog, and spends many days packing. She is also resourceful, burying the family silver in the garden so she can be sure it will be there on their return.

She feels no allegiance to Japan and has no difficulty passing the loyalty test that she is given in the internment camp. It is not that she has great patriotic feelings for the United States; she simply does not want to be sent back to Japan, and she wants to ensure that the family remains together. Since she lives in the United States, she wants to continue her life there.

In the internment camp she does her best to look after her children, but during the long cold winter she also gets worn down and depressed by the situation they are in. She does not bother to apply for any of the jobs that are available, and sometimes she just sits in her room doing nothing with an unopened book in her lap. She is haunted by the experience of having her husband suddenly taken from her with no explanation.

After she returns from the internment camp with the children, she must shoulder the responsibility of providing for her family. It will be several months before her husband returns, and he never works again. Facing prejudice because of her ethnicity, the mother is forced to take menial work cleaning houses. The work is hard and it ages her, but she does what she has to do for the sake of the family.

Elizabeth Morgan Roosevelt

Elizabeth Morgan Roosevelt is a young American girl with long yellow hair. She was a neighbor of the family that is sent to the internment camp. Elizabeth is a friend of the boy, and just before he goes away, she gives him a lucky stone from the sea. She writes to him at the camp, telling him all the news from Berkeley.

Son

The son is seven years old when the family is first sent to the internment camp. Like his sister, he is a typical young American; he likes baseball. However, in the months after Pearl Harbor before they are sent to the camp, he finds out what it is like to face discrimination because of his ethnicity. He learns to say that he is Chinese rather than Japanese so as to deflect this hostility. But on one occasion, having told a man he is Chinese, he runs to the corner of the street and shouts out that he is "Jap! Jap!"

The son is an impressionable young boy who absorbs a lot of information from his older sister, whom he asks a lot of questions. At the assembly center before they go to the camp, they stay in former horse stalls behind the racetrack, and after that the boy talks about horses a lot. He dreams he is riding a horse.

At the camp he misses his father badly and, at first, thinks he sees him everywhere among the other Japanese American men. His father had always been very affectionate toward him, calling him names like Little Guy and Gum Drop. The boy writes postcards to his father from the camp.

The boy seems to find it hard to adjust to life in the camp. Sometimes he lies awake at night listening to the radio bulletins about the war. Sometimes he wakes up from a bad dream wondering where he is. He wonders why he is in the camp and sometimes thinks it must be because he did something bad, but he never knows what that might have been. He keeps himself amused by playing marbles and Chinese checkers, and roaming around the barracks with the other boys, playing games. He keeps a pet tortoise in a wooden box filled with sand.

Themes

Prejudice

The Japanese Americans in the novel all face discrimination and prejudice based on their race. This becomes immediately apparent after the bombing of Pearl Harbor. The father is arrested and taken from his home at midnight even though he has done nothing wrong. He is not the only one. The boy hears of many other Japanese American fathers from the neighborhood who are arrested in similar fashion. Likewise, the families who are sent to the internment camps are innocent of wrongdoing. Many of them are U.S. citizens. Their only crime is to be of Japanese heritage. When some of the internees volunteer in the fall to work on farms in other states harvesting crops, they tell sad stories of prejudice when they return. Anti-Japanese sentiment is rampant, and they say they were shot at, spat upon, and refused entry to restaurants and movie theaters.

When the family returns to Berkeley after the war, they find the situation is much worse than before they left. No one welcomes them home, and people avoid them on the street. The children are picked on at school; their mother is unable to find anything other than menial work. The fear and dislike of Japanese Americans is typified by the employer who offers her a job only in a back room where no one will see her.

In spite of the prejudice they experience, the Japanese Americans are not shown reacting aggressively to it, even in their thoughts. They seem resigned to the situation. After their return, the children, for example, try to remain as inconspicuous as possible as long as the hostility continues. The only exception to this comes right at the end, when the father vents all his feelings of anger and frustration regarding the treatment he received.

Identity

The question of cultural identity is at the heart of the novel. The U.S. authorities assume that Japanese Americans are likely to side with their country of origin in the war, despite the lack of any evidence to support this notion. However, the mother, having lived in the United States for nearly twenty years, has no allegiance to the country of her birth. She has no difficulty in answering the loyalty questionnaire at the camp in a way that will keep her family together in the United States. She has no particular feelings of patriotism toward the United States, either; she just wants to keep the family together. Her lack of allegiance to Japan, however, does not mean that, as a first-generation immigrant, she does not retain some cultural ties to Japan. Before the order to evacuate comes, her home in Berkeley shows many signs of Japanese culture, including three silk kimonos she had brought with her from Japan, recordings of Japanese opera, a Japanese flag, and Imari dishes (Japanese porcelain). She feels compelled to destroy all these, however, to protect her family's safety. Not only does she feel the need to obliterate these signs of the family's Japanese origin, she even tells her children to deny their own heritage, just so they can stay safe. She instructs the children to say they are Chinese rather than Japanese.

There is a gap, though, between the first-generation immigrants such as the mother and father, who were born in Japan and retain something of their cultural origins, even if only in memory, and the second-generation Japanese Americans like the son and daughter who were born in the United States and know little of Japan. This is shown many times in the descriptions of the girl and boy. They are typical American children. The boy likes baseball and reads American comic books. The girl likes to leaf through the Sears, Roebuck catalog. The boy imagines himself fighting in the war on the American side and being awarded a Purple Heart by General MacArthur. He has seen American movies, and when he thinks of his father, knowing he has been branded as the enemy, he imagines him as an outlaw from a cowboy movie, wearing cowboy boots and a Stetson hat and riding a big horse. The other Japanese American boys also identify with the American side. Their war games in the camp include the chant *"Kill the Nazis! Kill the Japs!"*

Topics for Further Study

- What parallels are there between the situation faced by Japanese Americans in the 1940s and Muslims in the United States following the terrorist attacks in New York City and Washington, D.C., on September 11, 2001? In times of war or international terrorism, how should the U.S. government preserve the balance between homeland security and civil rights? What can we learn from the experience of Japanese American internment about how to treat U.S. citizens who belong to the same race or ethnic group as those who are attacking the United States? For example, how have Muslims and Arab Americans been treated since

September 11, 2001? Give a class presentation in which you discuss this important issue.

- Read *The Children of Topaz: The Story of a Japanese-American Internment Camp; Based on a Classroom Diary* (1996), by Michael O. Tunnell and George W. Chilcoat, which contains a real classroom diary kept by a thirdgrade class at the Topaz internment camp. Imagine that you have been interned somewhere in the United States because of some hostile situation in the country that has affected your race or ethnic group. Write some diary entries that describe your interests and concerns. What do you remember most from your life before internment? What do you miss most? What do you dream about? How do you spend your time? Upload your diary to your web log and share it with your classmates.

- Using Internet research, write an essay in which you discuss the typical differences between first-and second-generation immigrants to the United States. What sort of family issues are often raised when the parents were not born in the United

States but their children were? What kind of issues are raised regarding a person's sense of identity?

- It is often said that the United States is a nation of immigrants, but immigrants of many different races and ethnic groups have often faced hostility and discrimination when they first arrived here, and prejudice sometimes continued for several generations. Give a class presentation in which you briefly discuss the difficulties faced historically by German, Irish, Polish, Italian, and Jewish immigrants, as well as the more recent waves of immigrants from Asia and Central America. What are the economic, cultural, and racial factors that have contributed to the prejudice faced by immigrants?

Style

Point of View

The story is told from a variety of points of view. The first three chapters are told by a third-person narrator. Chapter 1 focuses on the point of view of the mother as she prepares the family for departure; chapter 2 is told from the point of view of the girl as the family travels on the train to Utah, and chapter 3, set in the internment camp, focuses mostly on the point of view of the boy—his thoughts, dreams, and impressions. The type of narration changes in chapter 4, which is narrated in the first-person plural ("we") by the two children after they return home from the camp. The last chapter is also a first-person narration, this time by the father. The changes in focus enable the author to present a well-rounded picture of how each member of the family copes with the experience of internment.

Setting

The setting reflects the lives of the main characters. The camp in Utah is a barren place high in the desert. There are no trees. It rarely rains in summer, and the wind is hot and dry. There is dust everywhere from the dust storms that go on for hours and sometimes days. Temperatures are extreme. In winter, the temperature sometimes drops to twenty degrees below zero. One late November, the men in the camp plant tree saplings that have been delivered, but the mother says the soil is too alkaline for them to last the winter, and she is proved correct. The barren terrain acts as a metaphor for the bleak lives lived by the internees.

The setting changes on the return of the family to California. Images of nature in full flower—a magnolia tree in bloom and hyacinths and narcissus in their garden—appear when they begin to be fully accepted again by the community in the spring of 1946. In May, the roses burst into bloom, and the children go searching for their mother's rosebush, which at some point was removed from where she had planted it in the front yard. The final image in that chapter is of the rosebush somewhere "blossoming madly, wildly, pressing one perfect flower after another out into the late afternoon light." Just as the desert landscape had suggested the empty nature of the lives the family was forced to endure, the rose image suggests that now the life force has reasserted itself and they can once more live full, happy lives.

Internment of Japanese Americans

After the surprise Japanese attack on the U.S. naval base at Pearl Harbor on December 7, 1941, the United States declared war on Japan and entered World War II. Japanese Americans immediately came under suspicion. It was thought that they might be loyal to Japan rather than to their adopted country and would act as spies or commit acts of sabotage. There had long been prejudice in the United States against Japanese immigrants. In 1924, for example, a law was passed that banned marriage between Japanese men and white women.

Compare & Contrast

- **1940s**: Japanese Americans face discrimination in the United States both during and after World War II.

  Today: As part of a larger group of Asian Americans, Japanese Americans have overcome past discrimination and are part of mainstream American society. They have made their mark in many fields of activity, including science and technology, literature and the arts, music, sports, and entertainment.

- **1940s**: According to the 1940 U.S. census, there are 126,947 Japanese Americans living in the United States. Of these, the vast majority live in the West, in California, Washington, and Oregon. Nearly two-thirds are U.S. citizens by birth.
  Today: According to the 2000 U.S. Census, there are 1,148,932 Japanese Americans in the United States, counting those who are Japanese American alone or in combination with one or more other races. Over 40 percent live in Hawaii or California.

- **1940s**: During World War II, Japan is an enemy of the United States. After the war, Japan is forced to accept U.S. occupation. The United States gives Japan a constitution, and the work of reconstructing the devastated nation begins.
  Today: Japan is a firm U.S. ally and the third-largest economy in the world, behind the United States and China.

Acting on these fears, President Franklin D. Roosevelt issued Executive Order 9066 on February 19, 1942. The Executive Order revoked the civil rights of Japanese Americans despite the fact that two-thirds of them were U.S. citizens. Nearly

120,000 Japanese Americans from all over the Pacific coast were rounded up and sent to ten internment camps built by the War Relocation Authority in seven states. Most of the camps were built in remote places on Native American reservations. The camps were surrounded by barbed wire, and armed guards prevented anyone from leaving.

Internment proved a catastrophic experience for Japanese Americans, who were forced to abandon their homes and businesses. They lost everything that they had worked for since coming to the United States, where many of them had lived for thirty or forty years. They were given no time to ensure the safe storage of their possessions, and when they departed for the camps, they were allowed to take only what they could physically carry.

The camps themselves had been hastily and poorly constructed along the lines of military barracks. They were unpleasant places to live and offered inadequate protection against extreme heat in summer and bitter cold in winter. Internees worked at low-paying jobs. Faced with such conditions, the internees made extensive efforts to build their own sense of community that would combat their isolation and the undignified manner in which they were compelled to live. They formed civic associations and created opportunities for entertainment such as dances, theatrical performances, and athletic events. There were also schools, which functioned with a minimum of equipment and books.

In January 1943, the U.S. government decided to recruit second-generation Japanese immigrants into an all–Japanese-American combat unit. All males in the internment camps were required to answer a series of questions, which included whether they were willing to serve in the U.S. armed forces and whether they would swear allegiance to the United States, defend the country against attack, and renounce obedience to the Japanese emperor. Most of the internees answered yes to these questions, but the several hundred who did not were sent to prison for disloyalty.

In 1944, the Supreme Court upheld Executive Order 9066, but the U.S. government finally rescinded it on January 2, 1945. All Japanese American prisoners were released from the internment camps, although it was some months before all of them were able to return to their homes. Some never made it back, since the U.S. government sent 4,724 Japanese Americans directly from the camps to Japan. Of these, 1,949 were U.S. citizens and almost all were under twenty years old. Some of them had expressed a desire for repatriation; others had renounced their U.S. citizenship.

Critical Overview

The novel received a number of favorable reviews. For Reba Leiding, in *Library Journal*, it is a "spare yet poignant first novel." Donna Seaman in *Booklist* commends the author, who "demonstrates a breathtaking restraint and delicacy throughout this supple and devastating first novel," in which she "universalizes [the characters'] experience of prejudice and disenfranchisement." The reviewer for *Publishers Weekly* comments, "The novel's honesty and matter-of-fact tone in the face of inconceivable injustice are the source of its power." *Kirkus Reviews* is less enthusiastic, acknowledging that the novel was "carefully researched" but arguing that it does not engage the reader emotionally: "The narrative remains stubbornly at the surface," detailing the injustices the detainees suffered, "but never finding a way to go deeper, to a place where the attention will be held rigid and the heart seized." Writing in the *New York Times Book Review*, Michael Upchurch has no such reservations. He calls it a "canny, muted first novel," and suggests that "Otsuka's portrait of the mother may be the book's greatest triumph. Almost everything in it is below the surface." Upchurch describes the "extraordinary" final chapter, in which the father speaks directly for the first time, as "a bitter tirade that is a burlesque version of what his supposed disloyalty would entail." What the reader is likely to notice most about the novel, in

Upchurch's view, is how much Otsuka is able to convey—in a line, in a paragraph—about her characters' surroundings, about their states of mind and about the mood of our country at a time of crisis that did not, on this particular front, bring out the best in its character.

What Do I Read Next?

- *The Buddha in the Attic* (2011) is Otsuka's widely praised second novel. It tells the story of the Japanese women who came to San Francisco in the early twentieth century to marry American men. They were known as "picture brides" because the exchange of photographs was the only contact they had had with the men they agreed to marry. The novel tells their story from their arrival in an alien culture to their gradual adaptation to American life, including raising children who identify more with America than with their Japanese heritage.

- *Snow Falling on Cedars* (1995) by David Guterson is set in the 1950s and centers around a murder trial on an isolated island north of Puget Sound, Washington. The defendant is a Japanese American fisherman, and the novel takes place in the shadow of the World War II internment of Japanese Americans and the prejudice they faced then, which continued into the 1950s. This celebrated novel won the PEN/Faulkner Award. The book has some sexual content and obscenities, which might make it unsuitable for middle-school readers.

- *Farewell to Manzanar* (1973) is a memoir by Jeanne Wakatsuki Houston. A seven-year-old American-born child in World War II, she was sent with her family to an internment camp for Japanese Americans at Manzanar, California. Dealing with issues such as prejudice, isolation, and cultural identity, the memoir captures the impact internment had on Houston's family and on other Japanese Americans.

- The fifteen stories in *Seventeen Syllables and Other Stories* (2001), by Hisaye Yamamoto, a second-generation Japanese American, cover a wide range of the Japanese American experience, from the internment camps during World War II to the tensions between first-generation and second-generation immigrants. Yamamoto's stories also emphasize the lives of women.

- First published in French in 1956, *Night*, by Elie Wiesel, is a memoir of Wiesel's experiences during the Holocaust. The story is told by Eliezar, a fourteen-year-old Jewish boy, beginning in Transylvania (now Romania) in 1941. In 1944, Eliezar and his family are sent to concentration camps, where the boy is witness to innumerable horrors. He is the only member of his family to survive. This memoir has long been regarded as one of the most compelling ever written by a Holocaust survivor. It appeared in a new translation by Marion Wiesel, Wiesel's wife, in 2006.

- *Ellen Levine's A Fence away from Freedom: Japanese Americans and*

World War II (1995) is a nonfiction book for young-adult readers about the internment of Japanese Americans. It consists of the testimonies of thirty-five people who were interned when they were children or adolescents. Their stories reveal what life in the camps was like and how people coped with it.

Sources

"About Julie Otsuka," Julie Otsuka website, http://www.julieotsuka.com/about/ (accessed December 4, 2011).

Bosworth, Allan R., *America's Concentration Camps*, W. W. Norton, 1967, p. 18.

Burton, J. M. Farrell, F. Lord, and R. Lord, "Topaz Relocation Center," in *Confinement and Ethnicity, an Overview of World War II Japanese American Relocation Sites*, http://www.cr.nps.gov/history/online_books/anthrop (accessed December 9, 2011).

"FDR and Japanese American Internment," Franklin D. Roosevelt Presidential Library and Museum website, http://www.fdrlibrary.marist.edu/archives/pdfs/intern (accessed December 9, 2011).

Gibson, Campbell, and Kay Jung, "Historical Census Statistics on Population Totals by Race, 1790 to 1990, and by Hispanic Origin, 1979 to 1990, for the United States, Regions, Divisions, and States," U.S. Department of Commerce website, Bureau of the Census, September 2002, http://www.census.gov/population/www/documentat (accessed December 5, 2011).

"Japan," in CIA: *World Fact Book*, 2011, https://www.cia.gov/library/publications/the-world-factbook/geos/ja.html (accessed December 5, 2011).

"Japanese American Demographics," Japanese American Citizens League website, http://www.jacl.org/about/Japanese_American_Dem (accessed December 5, 2011).

Kawano, Kelley, "A Conversation with Julie Otsuka," Random House website, http://www.randomhouse.com/boldtype/0902/otsuka (accessed December 4, 2011).

Leiding, Reba, Review of *When the Emperor Was Divine*, in *Library Journal*, Vol. 127, No. 14, September 1, 2002, p. 215.

"A More Perfect Union: Japanese Americans and the U.S. Constitution," Smithsonian Museum of American History website, http://americanhistory.si.edu/perfectunion/non-flash/overview.html (accessed December 5, 2011).

Nakayama, William, "Simmering Perfection," in *GoldSea*, http://goldsea.com/Personalities/Otsukaj/otsukaj.htm (accessed December 4, 2011).

Otsuka, Julie, *When the Emperor Was Divine*: A Novel, Knopf, 2002.

"Presidential Letter of Apology," PBS website, http://www.pbs.org/childofcamp/history/clinton.htm (accessed December 10, 2011).

Review of *When the Emperor Was Divine*, in *Kirkus Reviews*, August 1, 2002, p. 1068.

Review of *When the Emperor Was Divine*, in *Publishers Weekly*, Vol. 249, No. 34, August 26, 2002, p. 44.

Seaman, Donna, Review of *When the Emperor Was Divine*, in *Booklist*, Vol. 99, No. 1, September 1, 2002, p. 59.

"Topaz Camp," Topaz Museum website, http://www.topazmuseum.org/ (accessed December 4, 2011).

Upchurch, Michael, "The Last Roundup: A Novel about a Japanese-American Family Sent to a Relocation Camp during World War II," in *New York Times Book Review*, September 22, 2002, p. 14.

Further Reading

Cooper, Michael L., *Fighting for Honor: Japanese Americans and World War II*, Clarion Books, 2000.

> This is an account for young readers of the role played by Japanese Americans who joined the U.S. Army in World War II. More than 11,000 Japanese Americans fought in the 442nd Regimental Combat Team and many were decorated for their bravery. The book is based on diaries, autobiographies, and military records.

Daniels, Roger, *Prisoners without Trial: Japanese Americans in World War II*, Hill and Wang, 1993.

> This is a concise account of the incarceration of Japanese Americans during World War II. Daniels discusses topics such as the historical prejudice against Asian Americans, the upholding by the Supreme Court of the evacuation, life in the internment camps, and the difficulties involved in resettling internees after the war.

Taylor, Sandra C., *Jewel of the Desert: Japanese Internment at Topaz*, University of California Press, 1993.

Otsuka named this book as one she had found helpful in writing her novel. It tells the story of Japanese Americans from the San Francisco area who were interned at the camp in Topaz, Utah. The book includes interviews with fifty people who lived at the camp.

Uchida, Yoshiko, *Desert Exile: The Uprooting of a Japanese-American Family*, University of Washington Press, 1984.

Noted by Otsuka as one of the books she read and valued as she was writing her novel, this is an autobiographical narrative about how Uchida, her parents, and her sister were sent to an internment camp in Utah.

Suggested Search Terms

Julie Otsuka

Executive Order 9066

Japanese American internment

Japanese American internment AND Tanforan Racetrack

Pearl Harbor

Topaz internment camp

Nisei AND World War II

Kibei

Japanese American Redress Bill

No-No boys

Japanese American loyalty questionnaire

9 781375 396202